A GIFT FOR:

_____

FROM:

_____

EVERYTHING
I NEED TO KNOW
I LEARNED FROM
PEANUTS®

CHARLES M. SCHULZ

RUNNING PRESS
PHILADELPHIA · LONDON

Published in 2010 by Hallmark Gift Books, a division of Hallmark
Cards, Inc., under license from Running Press Book Publishers.

Visit us on the Web at Hallmark.com.

Designed by Jason Kayser
Edited by Cindy De La Hoz

ISBN 978-1-59530-318-9
BOK3105

Printed and bound in China.

Happy Birthday, Peanuts!

The year 2010 marks the Diamond Anniversary of Peanuts. Over the years Snoopy has taught us how to live life to the fullest, Lucy has taught us the wisdom of the ages through a unique brand of advanced psychiatry involving nickels, Linus has taught us that security can be found in a soft blue blankie, and we have worked out our worst fears and anxieties through good old Charlie Brown. In reviewing the evolution of Snoopy, Charlie Brown, Lucy, Linus, Peppermint Patty, Marcie, Schroeder, Rerun, and the rest of the gang, it becomes apparent that everything we need to know can be learned from Peanuts. They have given us a "How to" on just about every topic, pearls of wisdom to last a lifetime, and have pointed out what's most important for us. So grab a big slice of birthday cake and settle down to some of the best life lessons, as told by the wisest group of kindergarteners on the planet.

How to get the best seat
in the house . . .

OKAY, I GET THE HINT..
© 1992 United Feature Syndicate, Inc.
9-7
Z
SCHULZ

How to become
a golf pro...

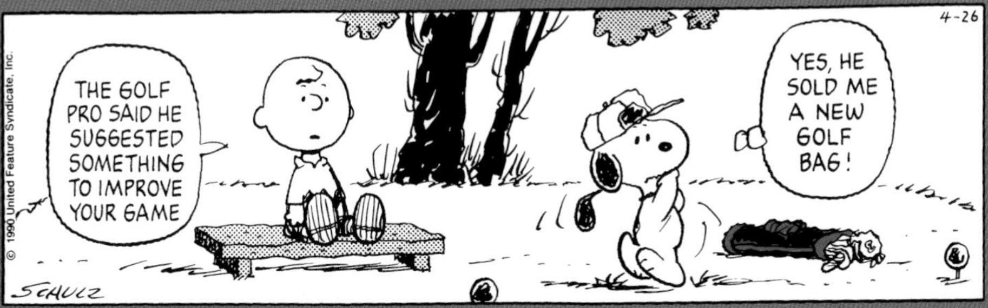
THE GOLF PRO SAID HE SUGGESTED SOMETHING TO IMPROVE YOUR GAME
YES, HE SOLD ME A NEW GOLF BAG!
4-26
SCHULZ

How to fight back...

LUCY SAID IF I NEED TWENTY-FIVE DOLLARS TO BUY PEGGY JEAN A CHRISTMAS PRESENT, I SHOULD SELL MY DOG...
© 1990 United Feature Syndicate, Inc.
WHAT A GREAT IDEA!
THAT'S THE FIRST TIME I'VE EVER SEEN HIM SPILL HIS WATER DISH..
12/6

A Pearl of Wisdom from

SNOOPY

I GAVE UP TRYING
TO UNDERSTAND PEOPLE
LONG AGO. NOW I
JUST LET THEM TRY TO
UNDERSTAND ME!

THE IMPORTANCE OF

Knowing When Enough
Is Enough

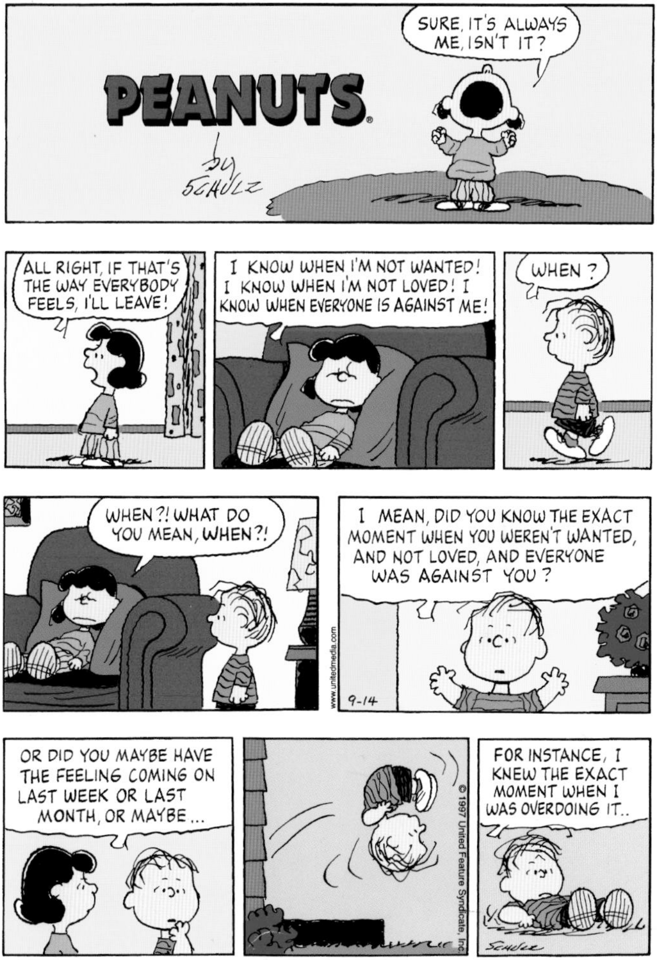
PEANUTS
by SCHULZ
SURE, IT'S ALWAYS ME, ISN'T IT?
ALL RIGHT, IF THAT'S THE WAY EVERYBODY FEELS, I'LL LEAVE!
I KNOW WHEN I'M NOT WANTED! I KNOW WHEN I'M NOT LOVED! I KNOW WHEN EVERYONE IS AGAINST ME!
WHEN ?
WHEN?! WHAT DO YOU MEAN, WHEN?!
www.unitedmedia.com
I MEAN, DID YOU KNOW THE EXACT MOMENT WHEN YOU WEREN'T WANTED, AND NOT LOVED, AND EVERYONE WAS AGAINST YOU?
9-14
OR DID YOU MAYBE HAVE THE FEELING COMING ON LAST WEEK OR LAST MONTH, OR MAYBE ...
© 1997 United Feature Syndicate, Inc.
FOR INSTANCE, I KNEW THE EXACT MOMENT WHEN I WAS OVERDOING IT..
SCHULZ

How to get to the root
of bible stories . . .

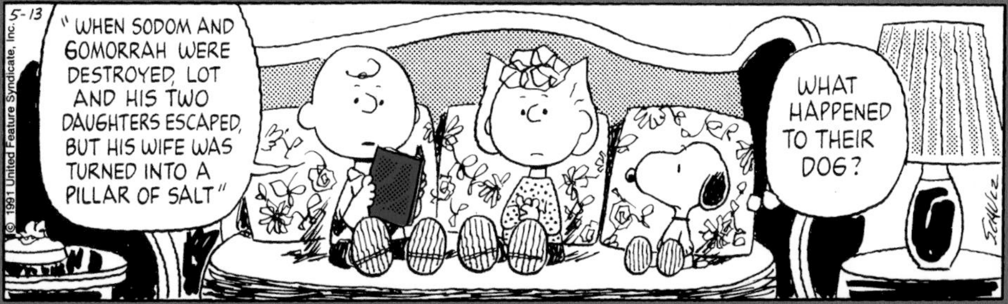
5-13
© 1991 United Feature Syndicate, Inc.
"WHEN SODOM AND GOMORRAH WERE DESTROYED, LOT AND HIS TWO DAUGHTERS ESCAPED, BUT HIS WIFE WAS TURNED INTO A PILLAR OF SALT"
WHAT HAPPENED TO THEIR DOG?
SCHULZ

How to make friends...

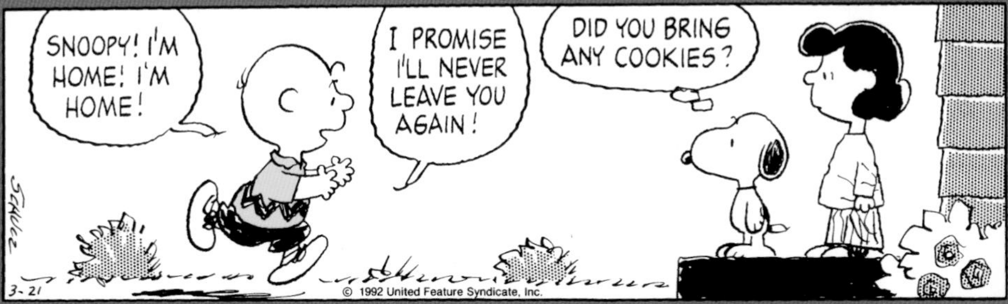
SNOOPY! I'M HOME! I'M HOME!
I PROMISE I'LL NEVER LEAVE YOU AGAIN!
DID YOU BRING ANY COOKIES?
SCHULZ
3-21
© 1992 United Feature Syndicate, Inc.

How to be profound . . .

SOMETIMES I WONDER HOW YOU CAN STAND BEING JUST A DOG..
10-4
© 1991 United Feature Syndicate, Inc.
YOU PLAY WITH THE CARDS YOU'RE DEALT..
WHATEVER THAT MEANS

A Pearl of Wisdom from

CHARLIE BROWN

THE SECRET OF HAPPINESS
IS HAVING THREE THINGS
TO LOOK FORWARD TO, AND
NOTHING TO DREAD!

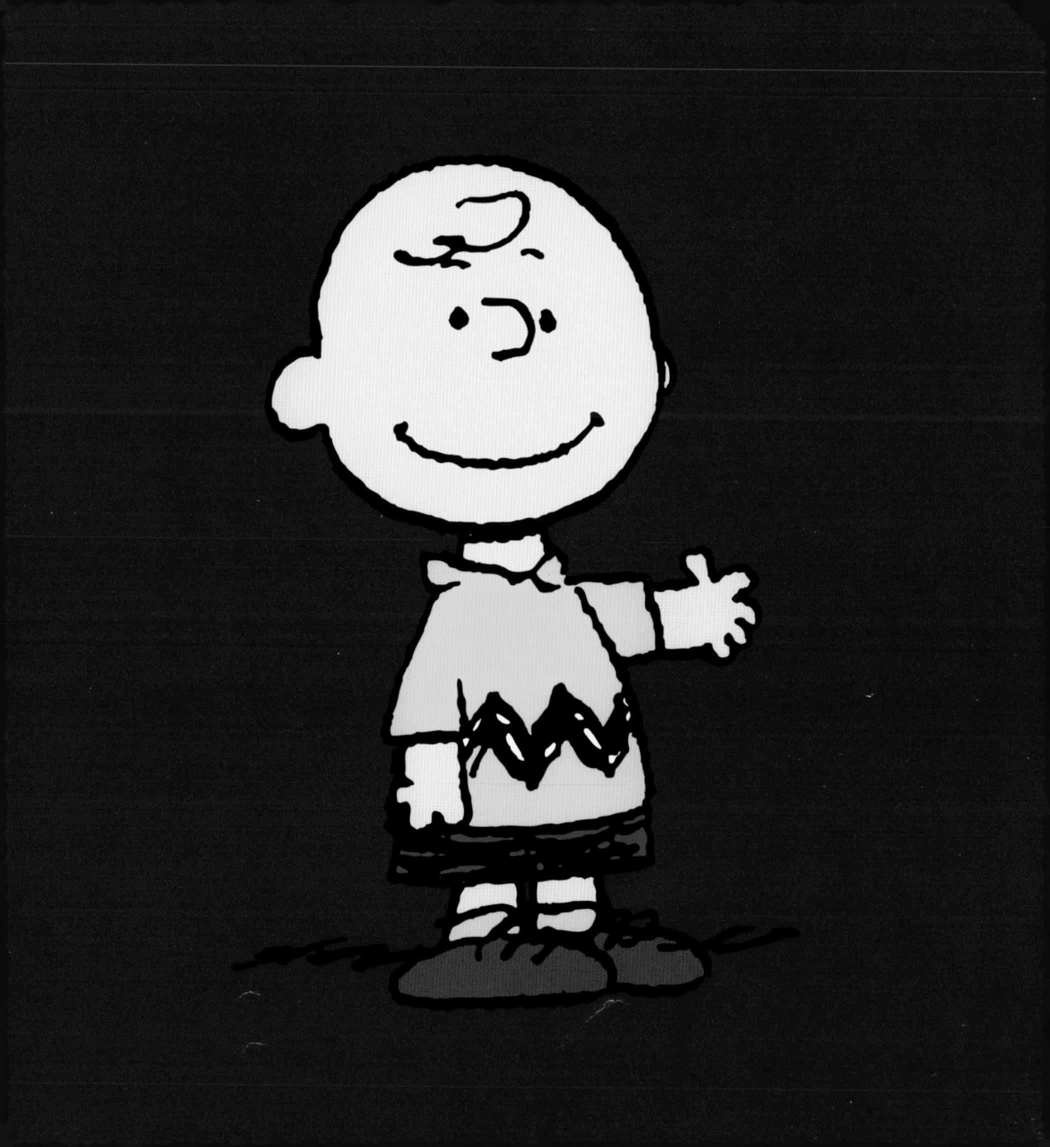

THE IMPORTANCE OF

Knowing the Rules of the Game

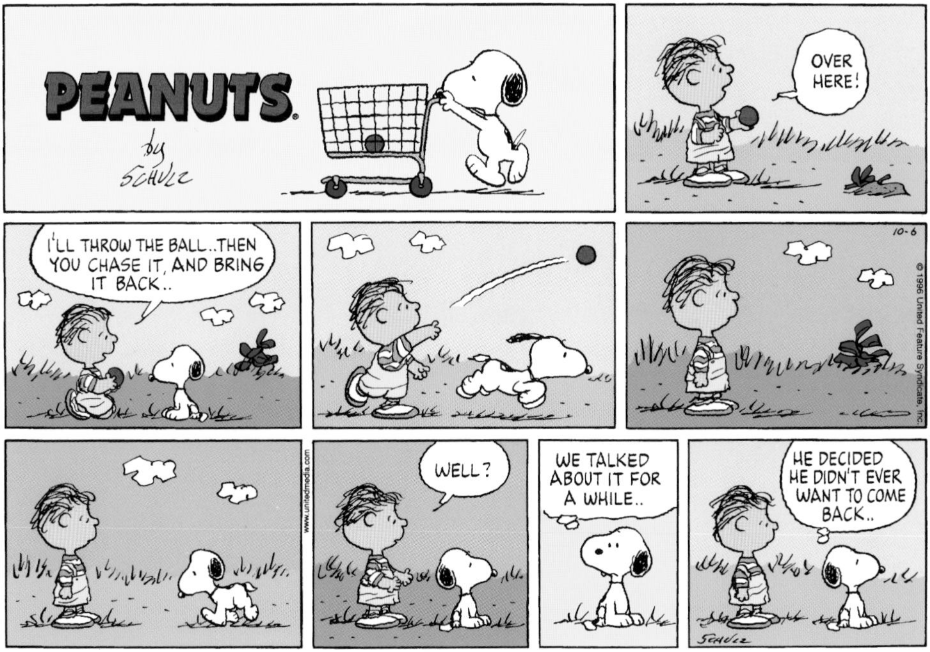
PEANUTS
by SCHULZ
OVER HERE!
I'LL THROW THE BALL..THEN YOU CHASE IT, AND BRING IT BACK..
10-6
© 1996 United Feature Syndicate, Inc.
www.unitedmedia.com
WELL?
WE TALKED ABOUT IT FOR A WHILE..
HE DECIDED HE DIDN'T EVER WANT TO COME BACK..
SCHULZ

How to earn brownie points
with your teacher . . .

MA'AM?
IS THERE ANYTHING I CAN DO TO EARN A LITTLE EXTRA CREDIT?
SHOVEL YOUR WALK?
© 1992 United Feature Syndicate, Inc.
12-7
SCHULZ

How to offend
a serious musician . . .

DID BEETHOVEN EVER PLAY "JINGLE BELLS"?
12-8
HE PROBABLY THOUGHT HE WAS TOO GOOD TO PLAY "JINGLE BELLS"
© 1992 United Feature Syndicate, Inc.
BONK!
IF I HAD BEEN THERE, I WOULD HAVE SAID, "HEY, LUDWIG, PLAY 'JINGLE BELLS'!"
SCHULZ

How to shop for
those difficult ones on your
Christmas list...

CHRISTMAS IS COMING.. I SHOULD START DOING MY SHOPPING..
12-15
LAST YEAR I EXCHANGED GIFTS WITH A ROCK.. I THINK HE LIKED WHAT I BOUGHT HIM...
© 1992 United Feature Syndicate, Inc.
HE'S STILL WEARING IT..
SCHULZ

LUCY

THE WORLD CAN'T COME
TO AN END TODAY
BECAUSE IT IS ALREADY
TOMORROW IN SOME OTHER
PART OF THE WORLD!

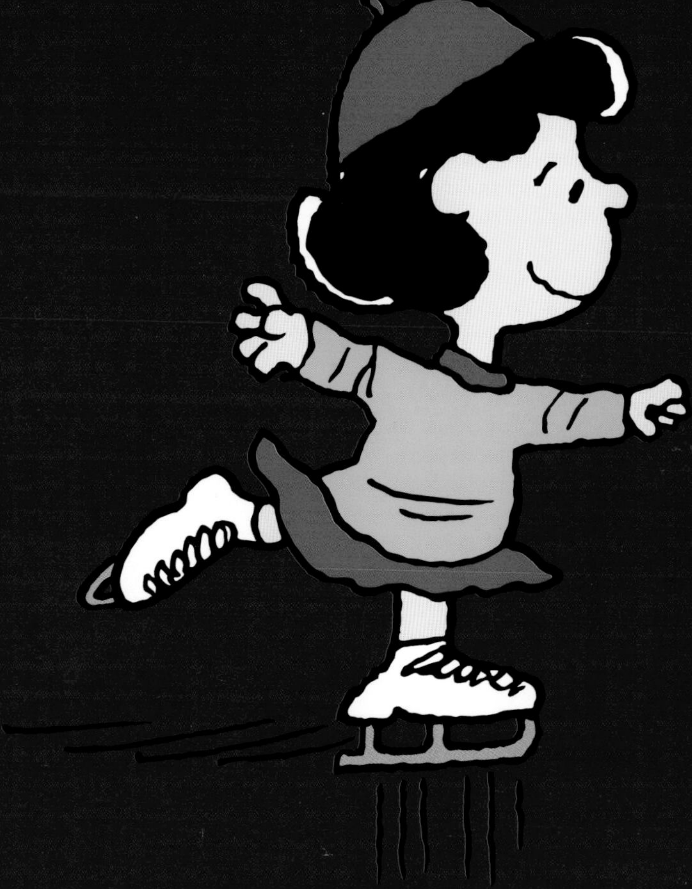

THE IMPORTANCE OF

Nature in Solving Life's Problems

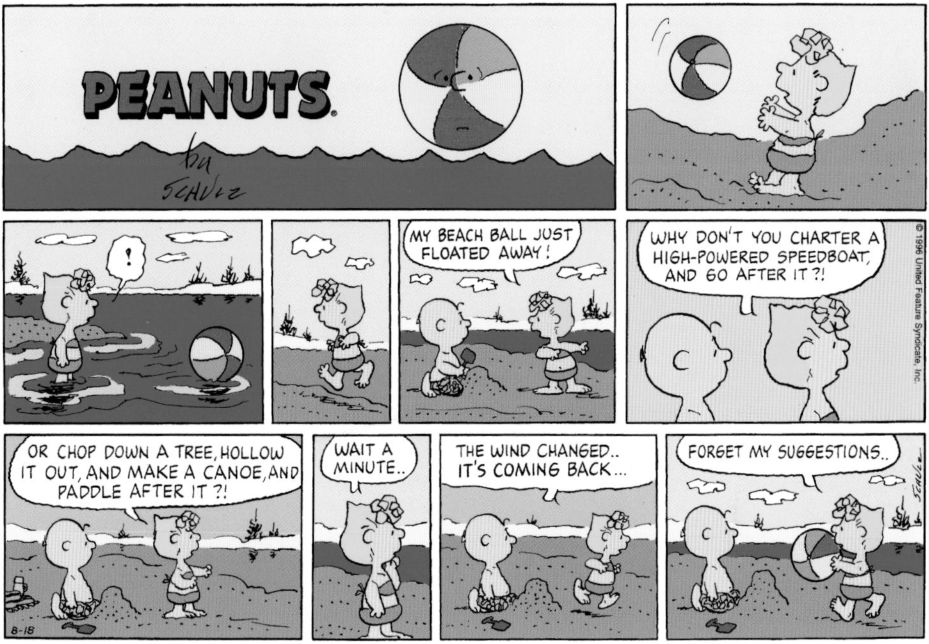
PEANUTS
by SCHULZ
!
MY BEACH BALL JUST FLOATED AWAY!
WHY DON'T YOU CHARTER A HIGH-POWERED SPEEDBOAT, AND GO AFTER IT?!
© 1996 United Feature Syndicate, Inc.
OR CHOP DOWN A TREE, HOLLOW IT OUT, AND MAKE A CANOE, AND PADDLE AFTER IT?!
8-18
WAIT A MINUTE..
THE WIND CHANGED.. IT'S COMING BACK...
FORGET MY SUGGESTIONS..
SCHULZ

How to spend
that post-retirement
spare time . . .

1-30
MY GRAMPA SAYS HE TAKES ONE HUNDRED AND FOUR STROKES WITH HIS RAZOR WHEN HE SHAVES..
© 1993 United Feature Syndicate, Inc.
HE COUNTED THEM?
GRAMPA IS RETIRED.. HE DOESN'T HAVE MUCH ELSE TO DO..
SCHULZ

How to be a team leader...

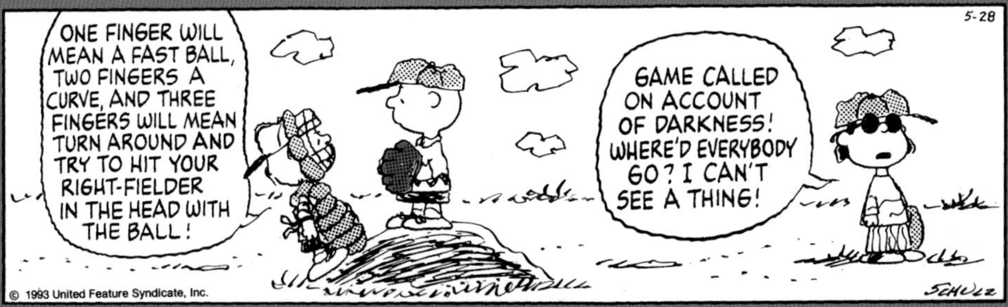
5-28
ONE FINGER WILL MEAN A FAST BALL, TWO FINGERS A CURVE, AND THREE FINGERS WILL MEAN TURN AROUND AND TRY TO HIT YOUR RIGHT-FIELDER IN THE HEAD WITH THE BALL!
GAME CALLED ON ACCOUNT OF DARKNESS! WHERE'D EVERYBODY GO? I CAN'T SEE A THING!
© 1993 United Feature Syndicate, Inc.
SCHULZ

How the circle of
life turns . . .

WHEN YOU DIE, ARE YOU EVER ALLOWED TO COME BACK?
ONLY IF YOU HAD YOUR HAND STAMPED..
5-31
SCHULZ

A Pearl of Wisdom from

LINUS

NEVER SET YOUR STOMACH
FOR A JELLY-BREAD
SANDWICH UNTIL YOU'RE
SURE THERE'S SOME JELLY!

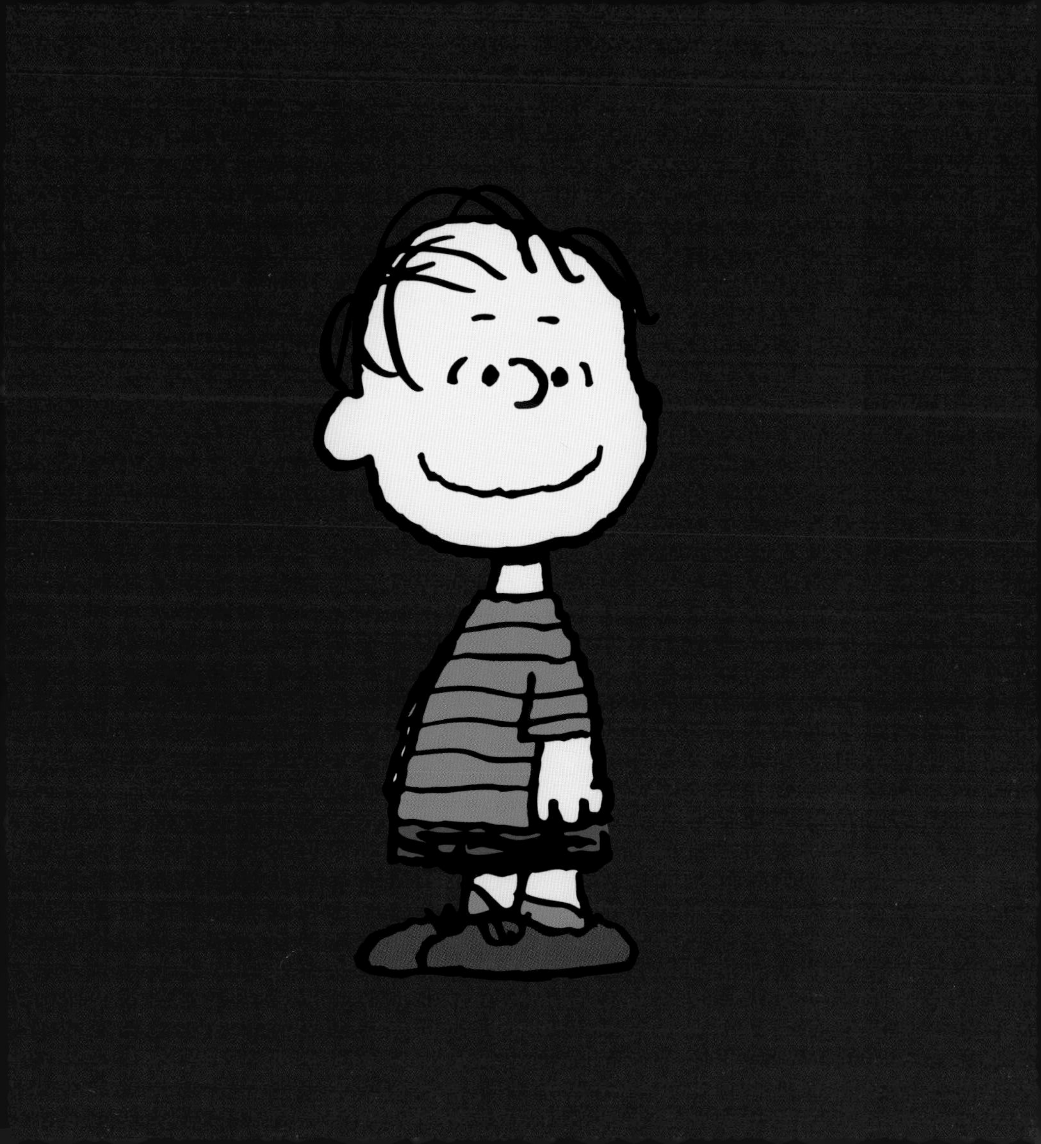

THE IMPORTANCE OF

Perseverance

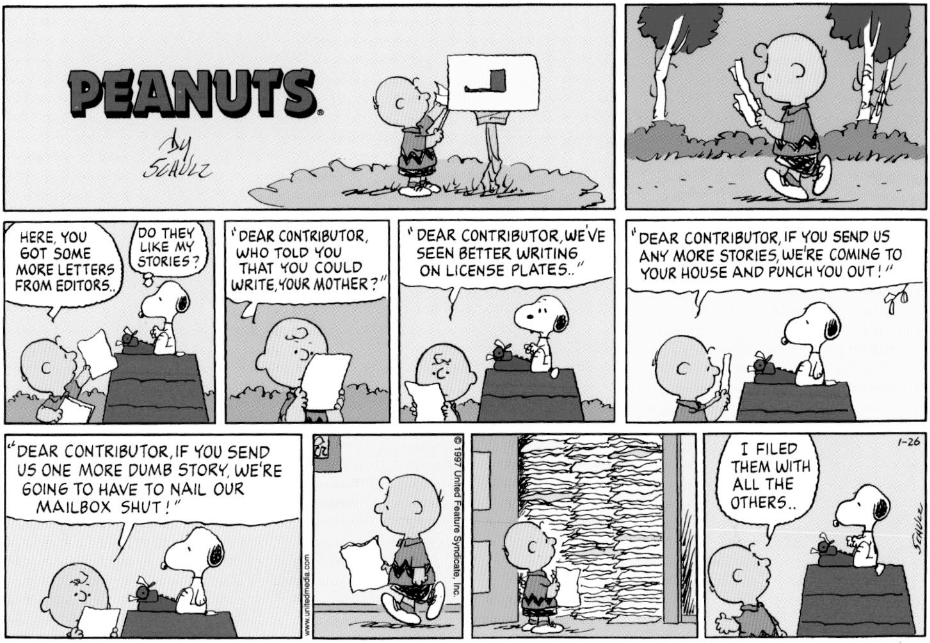
PEANUTS
by SCHULZ
HERE, YOU GOT SOME MORE LETTERS FROM EDITORS..
DO THEY LIKE MY STORIES?
"DEAR CONTRIBUTOR, WHO TOLD YOU THAT YOU COULD WRITE, YOUR MOTHER?"
"DEAR CONTRIBUTOR, WE'VE SEEN BETTER WRITING ON LICENSE PLATES.."
"DEAR CONTRIBUTOR, IF YOU SEND US ANY MORE STORIES, WE'RE COMING TO YOUR HOUSE AND PUNCH YOU OUT!"
"DEAR CONTRIBUTOR, IF YOU SEND US ONE MORE DUMB STORY, WE'RE GOING TO HAVE TO NAIL OUR MAILBOX SHUT!"
© 1997 United Feature Syndicate, Inc.
www.unitedmedia.com
1-26
I FILED THEM WITH ALL THE OTHERS..
SCHULZ

How to be tactful . . .

JUST SAY, "FAULT."
YOU DON'T HAVE TO SAY, "LOUSY FIRST SERVE"
© 1990 United Feature Syndicate, Inc.
SCHULZ
8-18

How to win a girl's heart...

I JUST DON'T KNOW HOW TO WRITE A LOVE LETTER
WHAT CAN YOU SAY TO A GIRL THAT SHOWS YOU REALLY LIKE HER?
HOW ABOUT, "ENCLOSED PLEASE FIND A COOKIE"?
© 1990 United Feature Syndicate, Inc.
SCHULZ
8-20

How to make up excuses
for skipping class . . .

ARE YOU GOING TO SUNDAY SCHOOL TOMORROW ?
© 1990 United Feature Syndicate, Inc.
I GUESS SO.. WHY?
THE TEACHER WANTED TO KNOW WHY YOU WEREN'T THERE LAST SUNDAY..
12-15
THE ZIPPER ON MY BIBLE WAS STUCK..
SCHULZ

A Pearl of Wisdom from

PEPPERMINT
PATTY

NEVER GIVE YOUR HEART
TO A BLOCKHEAD.

THE IMPORTANCE OF

Technology

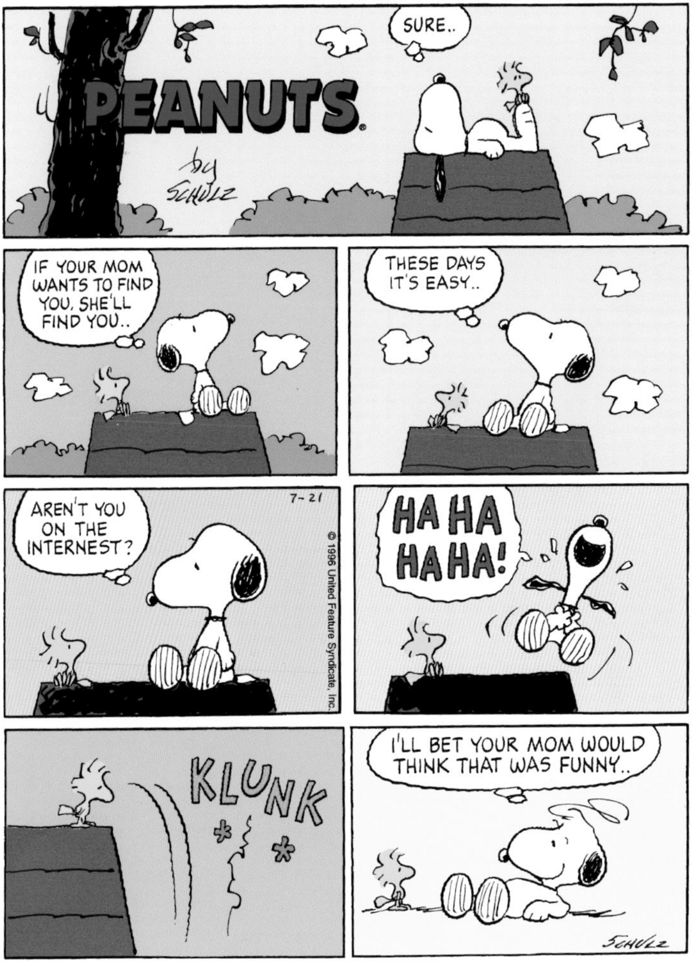
PEANUTS
by SCHULZ
SURE..
IF YOUR MOM WANTS TO FIND YOU, SHE'LL FIND YOU..
THESE DAYS IT'S EASY..
7-21
AREN'T YOU ON THE INTERNEST?
© 1996 United Feature Syndicate, Inc.
HA HA HA HA!
KLUNK
I'LL BET YOUR MOM WOULD THINK THAT WAS FUNNY..
SCHULZ

How to be a success...

THEY SAY THE SECRET OF SUCCESS IS TO GET UP EARLY IN THE MORNING..
SO?
I'M UP!
12-21
© 1992 United Feature Syndicate, Inc.
SCHULZ

How to cope when you've forgotten your umbrella...

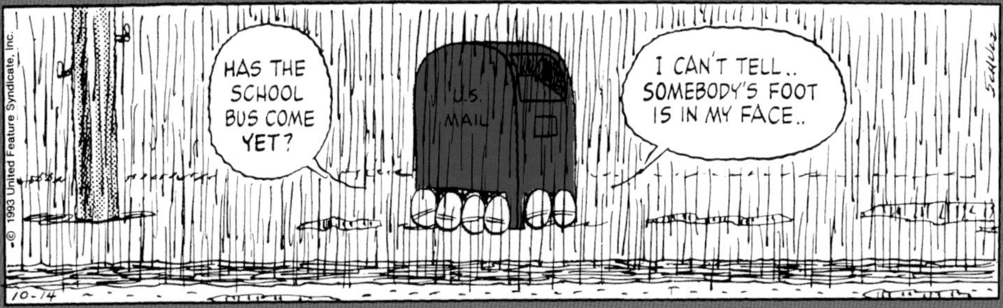
HAS THE SCHOOL BUS COME YET?
I CAN'T TELL.. SOMEBODY'S FOOT IS IN MY FACE..
U.S. MAIL
SCHULZ
10-14

How to recharge
after a workout...

I SUPPOSE A LONG-DISTANCE RUNNER LIKE YOURSELF WATCHES WHAT HE EATS..
ABSOLUTELY
6-5
© 1993 United Feature Syndicate, Inc.
AFTER I'M DONE, I ALWAYS EAT A POWER DOUGHNUT..
SCHULZ

A Pearl of Wisdom from

PIGPEN

THE WORLD NEEDS
MESSY PEOPLE . . .
OTHERWISE THE NEAT
PEOPLE WOULD TAKE OVER!

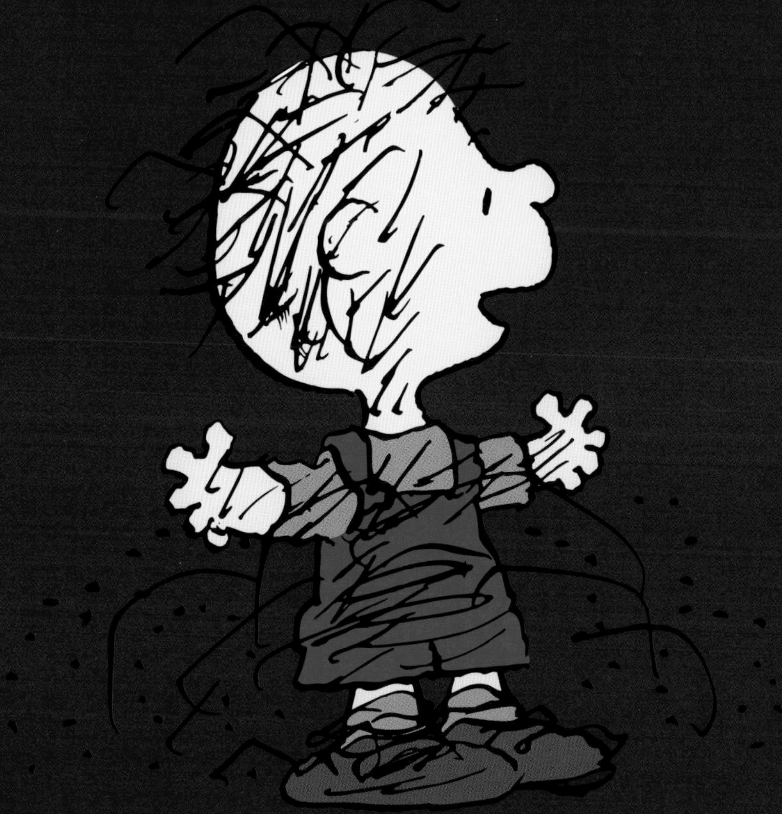

THE IMPORTANCE OF

Having a Good Attorney

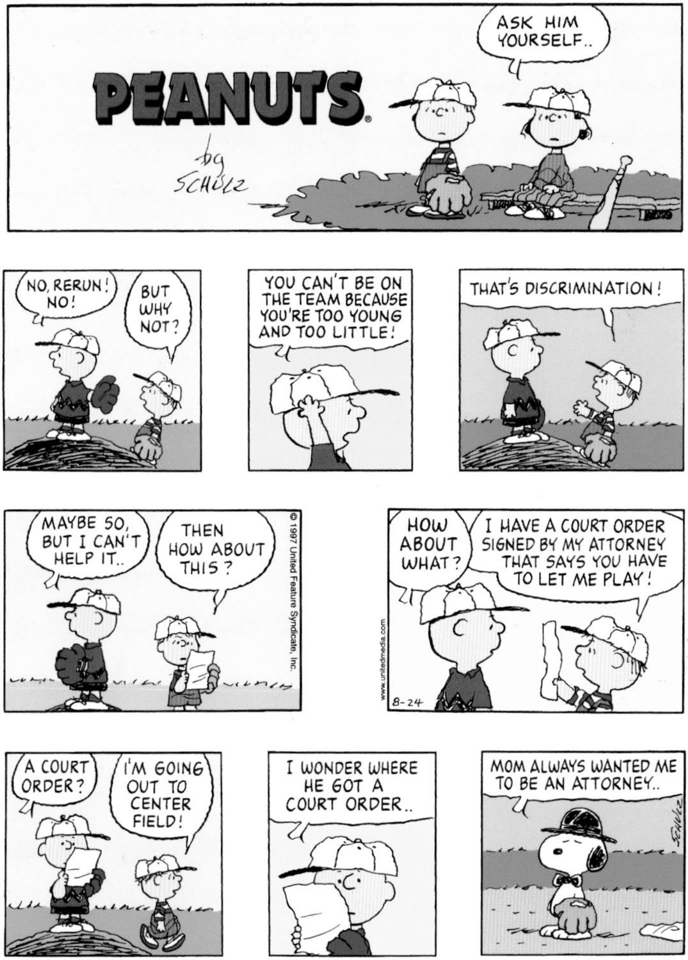
PEANUTS
by SCHULZ
ASK HIM YOURSELF..
NO, RERUN! NO!
BUT WHY NOT?
YOU CAN'T BE ON THE TEAM BECAUSE YOU'RE TOO YOUNG AND TOO LITTLE!
THAT'S DISCRIMINATION!
MAYBE SO, BUT I CAN'T HELP IT..
THEN HOW ABOUT THIS?
© 1997 United Feature Syndicate, Inc.
www.unitedmedia.com
HOW ABOUT WHAT?
I HAVE A COURT ORDER SIGNED BY MY ATTORNEY THAT SAYS YOU HAVE TO LET ME PLAY!
8-24
A COURT ORDER?
I'M GOING OUT TO CENTER FIELD!
I WONDER WHERE HE GOT A COURT ORDER..
MOM ALWAYS WANTED ME TO BE AN ATTORNEY..
SCHULZ

How to get a free meal…

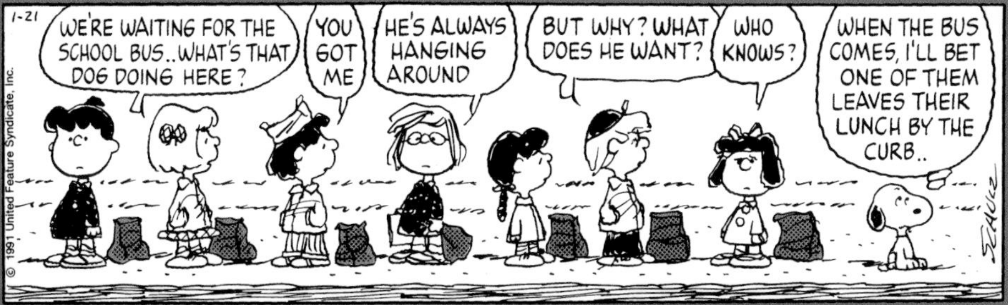
1-21
WE'RE WAITING FOR THE SCHOOL BUS..WHAT'S THAT DOG DOING HERE ?
YOU GOT ME
HE'S ALWAYS HANGING AROUND
BUT WHY? WHAT DOES HE WANT?
WHO KNOWS?
WHEN THE BUS COMES, I'LL BET ONE OF THEM LEAVES THEIR LUNCH BY THE CURB..
© 1991 United Feature Syndicate, Inc.
SCHULZ

How to listen
to your body…

PEANUTS
MY STOMACH TELLS ME IT'S SUPPERTIME
RATS!
IT ISN'T EVEN NEAR SUPPERTIME...
I HATE HAVING A STOMACH THAT TELLS LIES!
3-27
SCHULZ
Tm. Reg. U. S. Pat. Off.—All rights reserved
© 1965 by United Feature Syndicate, Inc.

How to accept
constructive criticism . . .

From the day I was born my life has been hard.
THIS IS RIDICULOUS! YOU HAVE AN EASY LIFE!
5-16
© 1994 United Feature Syndicate, Inc.
Starting now, my life has been very hard.
SCHULZ

A Pearl of Wisdom from

SALLY

WHO CARES WHAT OTHER
PEOPLE THINK?

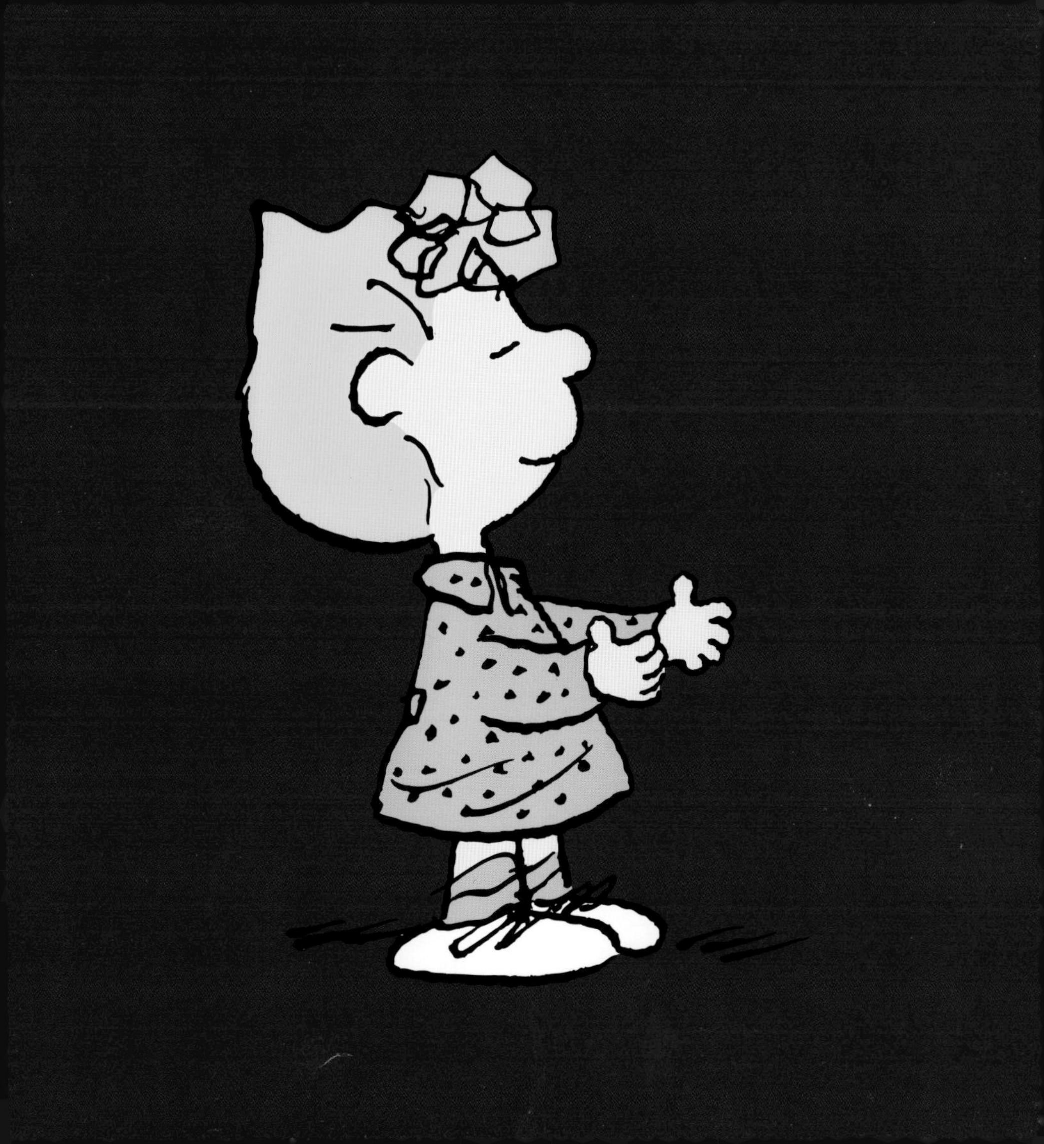

THE IMPORTANCE OF

Having the Right Answers

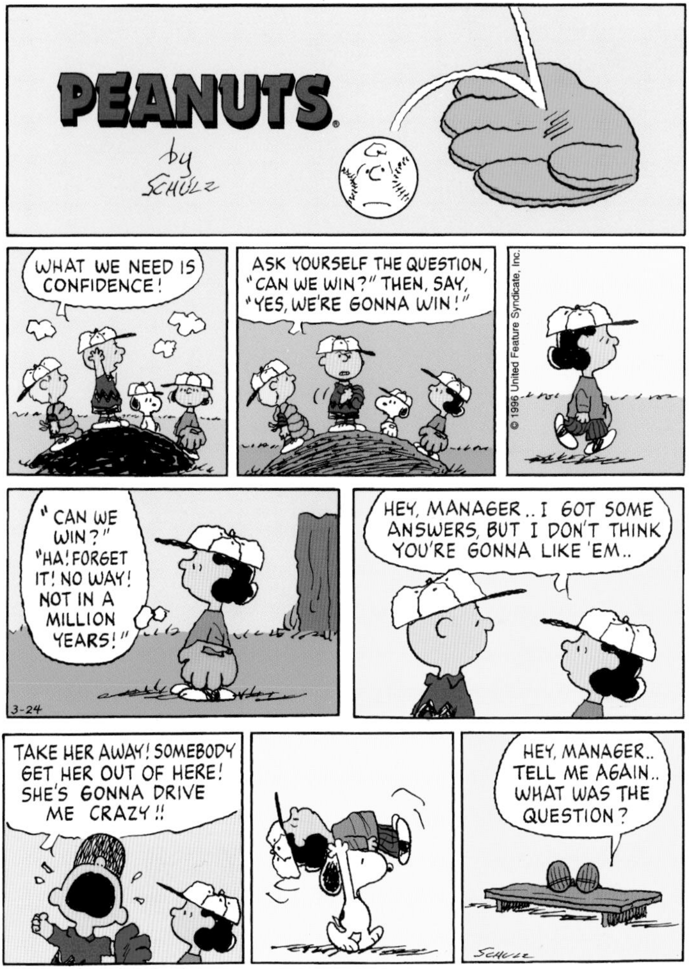
PEANUTS
by SCHULZ
WHAT WE NEED IS CONFIDENCE!
ASK YOURSELF THE QUESTION, "CAN WE WIN?" THEN, SAY, "YES, WE'RE GONNA WIN!"
© 1996 United Feature Syndicate, Inc.
"CAN WE WIN?" "HA! FORGET IT! NO WAY! NOT IN A MILLION YEARS!"
3-24
HEY, MANAGER.. I GOT SOME ANSWERS, BUT I DON'T THINK YOU'RE GONNA LIKE 'EM..
TAKE HER AWAY! SOMEBODY GET HER OUT OF HERE! SHE'S GONNA DRIVE ME CRAZY!!
HEY, MANAGER.. TELL ME AGAIN.. WHAT WAS THE QUESTION?
SCHULZ

How to learn
from our elders...

YOU'VE TIED YOUR OWN SHOES, RERUN! GOOD FOR YOU
NOW, OF COURSE, THERE'S ONE OTHER THING...
2-26
THE SOCKS GO ON BEFORE THE SHOES..
© 1994 United Feature Syndicate, Inc.
SCHULZ

How to have
a good conversation . . .

IN A GOOD CONVERSATION, ONE PERSON TALKS WHILE THE OTHER LISTENS
THEN THAT PERSON TALKS WHILE THE FIRST PERSON LISTENS...
I LIKE TALKING.. I HATE LISTENING
I REALIZE THAT
WHAT ?
3-2
SCHULZ
© 1985 United Feature Syndicate, Inc.

How to get a guy...

I FEEL GOOD TODAY!
I FEEL I CAN CATCH ANYTHING THAT COMES MY WAY!
4-11
© 1985 United Feature Syndicate, Inc.
HEY, SWEETIE, YOU COMING MY WAY?
SCHULZ

A Pearl of Wisdom from

THE FLYING ACE

ITS EITHER THE FLU
OR LOVE ... THE SYMPTOMS
ARE THE SAME.

THE IMPORTANCE OF

Having a Dog

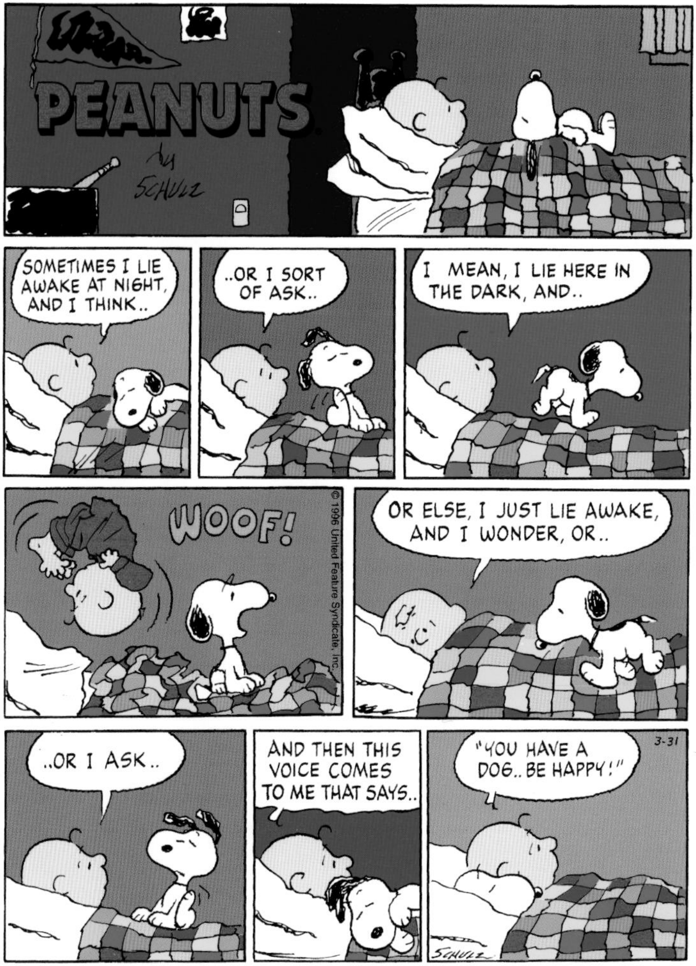
PEANUTS
by SCHULZ
SOMETIMES I LIE AWAKE AT NIGHT, AND I THINK..
..OR I SORT OF ASK..
I MEAN, I LIE HERE IN THE DARK, AND..
WOOF!
© 1996 United Feature Syndicate, Inc.
OR ELSE, I JUST LIE AWAKE, AND I WONDER, OR..
..OR I ASK..
AND THEN THIS VOICE COMES TO ME THAT SAYS..
"YOU HAVE A DOG.. BE HAPPY!"
3-31
SCHULZ

How to know when
a relationship is
going nowhere...

DO YOU MIND IF I ASK YOU SOMETHING?

WHAT DO YOU REALLY THINK THE CHANCES ARE THAT YOU AND I WILL GET MARRIED SOMEDAY?

WELL, LET ME SEE... HOW CAN I PUT IT?

WHEN SOMEONE DOESN'T KNOW HOW TO PUT IT, YOU KNOW YOU'VE BEEN PUT!

© 1985 United Feature Syndicate, Inc.

How to bargain . . .

PSYCHIATRIC HELP 5¢
THE DOCTOR IS IN
THINK ABOUT WHAT I'VE SAID, CHARLIE BROWN
IT'S REALLY ALL UP TO YOU..
11-14
FIVE CENTS, PLEASE
DO YOU TAKE BUBBLE GUM CARDS?
© 1986 United Feature Syndicate, Inc.
SCHULZ

How to get famous…

PSYCHIATRIC HELP 5¢
LET ME GET THIS STRAIGHT..
THE DOCTOR IS IN
YOU WERE HANGING UPSIDE DOWN FROM A TREE, AND YOU SAW THE TREE EAT YOUR KITE...
IT WAS A KITE-EATING TREE
6-1
© 1987 United Feature Syndicate, Inc.
I'D BETTER TAKE NOTES.. THIS CASE COULD MAKE ME FAMOUS!
THE DOCTOR IS IN
SCHULZ

A Pearl of Wisdom from

MARCIE

WAKE UP AND SMELL
THE BUBBLE GUM.

THE IMPORTANCE OF

Humility

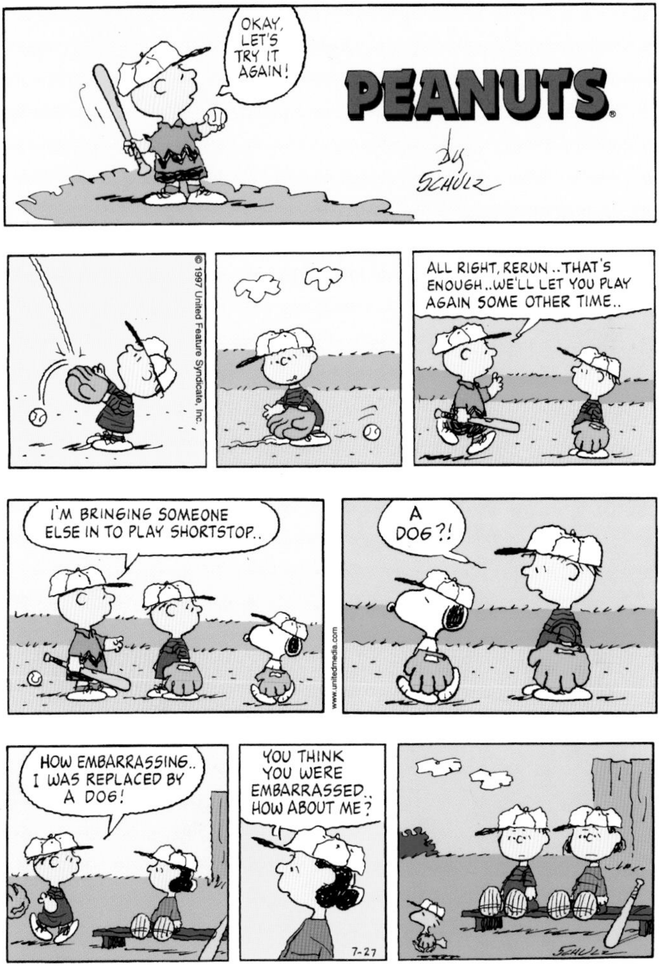
OKAY, LET'S TRY IT AGAIN!
PEANUTS
by SCHULZ
© 1997 United Feature Syndicate, Inc.
ALL RIGHT, RERUN..THAT'S ENOUGH..WE'LL LET YOU PLAY AGAIN SOME OTHER TIME..
I'M BRINGING SOMEONE ELSE IN TO PLAY SHORTSTOP..
www.unitedmedia.com
A DOG?!
HOW EMBARRASSING.. I WAS REPLACED BY A DOG!
YOU THINK YOU WERE EMBARRASSED.. HOW ABOUT ME?
7-27
SCHULZ

How to deal
with censorship . . .

I'M OUR SCHOOL BOOK REVIEWER
I NEED TO CHECK YOUR NOVEL TO SEE IF IT'S SUITABLE FOR OUR SCHOOL LIBRARY...
"Rats!" cried the hero.
© 1985 United Feature Syndicate, Inc.
10-16
"CONTAINS MILD PROFANITY.."
SCHULZ

How to shut people up . . .

WHAT MAKES YOU THINK YOU HAVE THE ANSWERS FOR EVERYTHING?
WHAT ABOUT THE REST OF US? HOW DO YOU THINK YOU'RE GOING TO KEEP THE REST OF US FROM EXPRESSING AN OPINION?
© 1988 United Feature Syndicate, Inc.
SCHULZ
10-7

How to eat ice cream . . .

I ALWAYS HAVE THE VANILLA ON THE BOTTOM AND THE CHOCOLATE ON TOP
YOU LIKE TO HAVE THE VANILLA ON TOP AND THE CHOCOLATE ON THE BOTTOM?
2-8
THAT'S INTERESTING..
© 1986 United Feature Syndicate, Inc.
IT TAKES ALL KINDS TO MAKE A WORLD!
SCHULZ

A Pearl of Wisdom from

RERUN

I'VE LEARNED ALL
I NEED TO KNOW TO LIVE
UNDER A BED.

THE IMPORTANCE OF

Making Yourself at Home

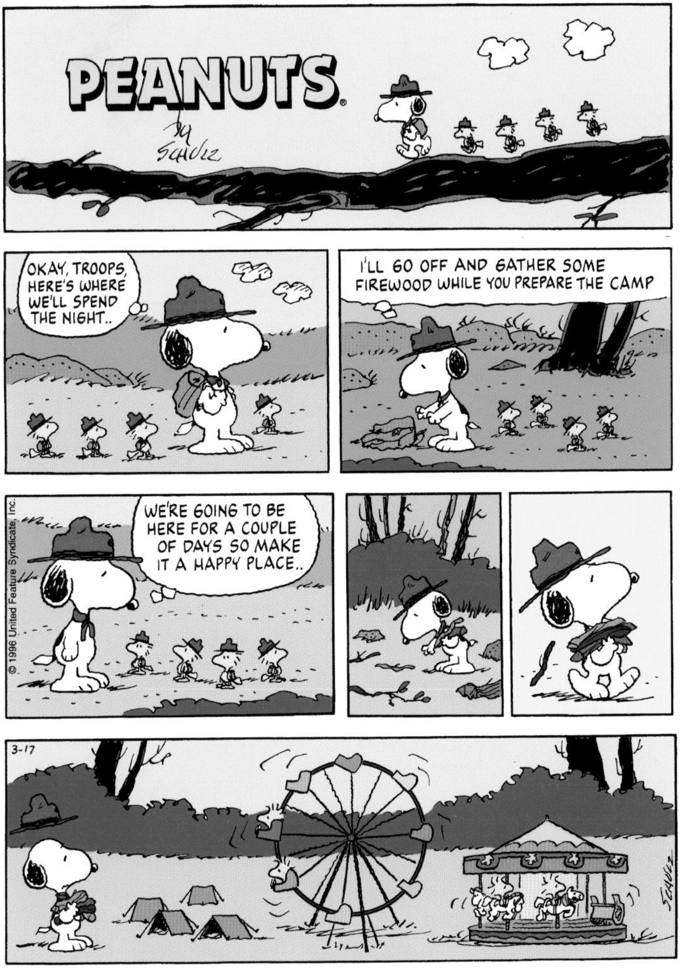
PEANUTS
SCHULZ
OKAY, TROOPS, HERE'S WHERE WE'LL SPEND THE NIGHT..
I'LL GO OFF AND GATHER SOME FIREWOOD WHILE YOU PREPARE THE CAMP
© 1996 United Feature Syndicate, Inc.
WE'RE GOING TO BE HERE FOR A COUPLE OF DAYS SO MAKE IT A HAPPY PLACE..
3-17
SCHULZ

How to appear intelligent...

YES, MA'AM? CHARLES DICKENS!
11-23
SIR, HOW DID YOU KNOW THAT?
IF YOU GO TO SCHOOL LONG ENOUGH, SOONER OR LATER THE ANSWER IS GOING TO BE CHARLES DICKENS..
SCHULZ
© 1994 United Feature Syndicate, Inc.

How to avoid
difficult questions . . .

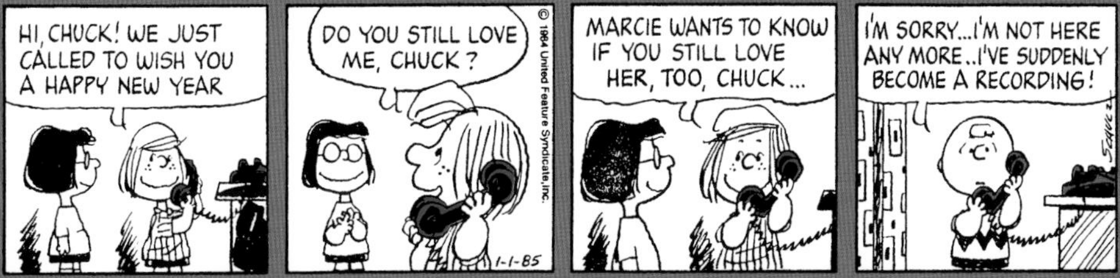
HI, CHUCK! WE JUST CALLED TO WISH YOU A HAPPY NEW YEAR
DO YOU STILL LOVE ME, CHUCK?
© 1984 United Feature Syndicate, Inc.
1-1-85
MARCIE WANTS TO KNOW IF YOU STILL LOVE HER, TOO, CHUCK...
I'M SORRY...I'M NOT HERE ANY MORE..I'VE SUDDENLY BECOME A RECORDING!
SCHULZ

How to make a person
uncomfortable . . .

I CAN'T SHARE THIS WITH YOU.. THEY SAY ICE CREAM ISN'T GOOD FOR DOGS...
© 1991 United Feature Syndicate, Inc.
AND IF YOU STARE AT ME LIKE THAT, YOU'RE GOING TO SPOIL IT FOR ME..
6-21
I'LL SETTLE FOR THAT
SCHULZ

SCHROEDER

———————

TO ME, LOVE SONGS
ARE LIKE EATING
TOO MUCH ICE CREAM.

THE IMPORTANCE OF

Helping a Friend ... Or at Least Trying to

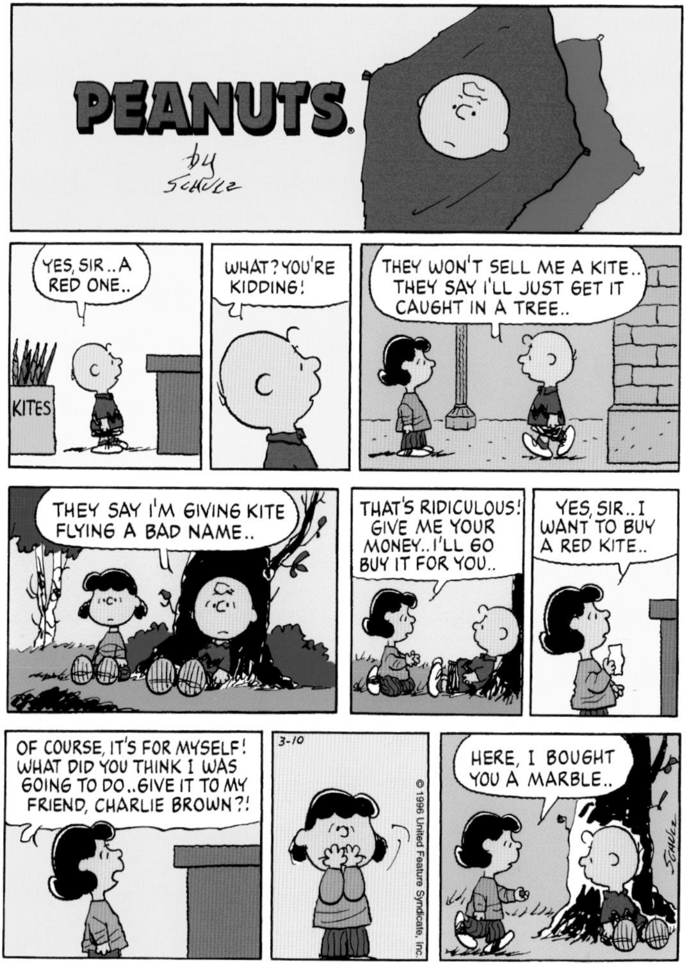
PEANUTS
by SCHULZ
YES, SIR .. A RED ONE..
KITES
WHAT? YOU'RE KIDDING!
THEY WON'T SELL ME A KITE.. THEY SAY I'LL JUST GET IT CAUGHT IN A TREE..
THEY SAY I'M GIVING KITE FLYING A BAD NAME..
THAT'S RIDICULOUS! GIVE ME YOUR MONEY.. I'LL GO BUY IT FOR YOU..
YES, SIR.. I WANT TO BUY A RED KITE..
OF COURSE, IT'S FOR MYSELF! WHAT DID YOU THINK I WAS GOING TO DO..GIVE IT TO MY FRIEND, CHARLIE BROWN?!
3-10
© 1996 United Feature Syndicate, Inc.
HERE, I BOUGHT YOU A MARBLE..
SCHULZ

How to get work done
in a pinch...

I CAN'T HELP YOU WITH YOUR HOMEWORK TONIGHT.. I'M TOO TIRED...
THAT'S ALL RIGHT.. IT'LL WORK OUT FINE...
I'LL PUT DOWN THE SAME TIRED OLD ANSWERS TO THE SAME TIRED OLD QUESTIONS
SCHULZ
4-24
© 1992 United Feature Syndicate, Inc.

How to find security . . .

WHEN I HEAR THOSE COYOTES HOWLING AT NIGHT, IT TOTALLY DEPRESSES ME..
I START TO FEEL LONELY...THEN I GET SCARED...
© 1992 United Feature Syndicate, Inc.
I THOUGHT HOLDING ONTO THAT BLANKET MADE YOU SECURE..
I THINK THE WARRANTY HAS RUN OUT..
SCHULZ
8-27

How to fake it . . .

WE'RE SUPPOSED TO BE READING "THE BROTHERS KARAMAZOV," CHUCK.. CAN YOU TELL ME ABOUT IT?
WELL, THERE ARE THESE THREE BROTHERS, SEE, AND...
THREE, HUH? THANKS, CHUCK.. I CAN FAKE THE REST..
5-14

A Pearl of Wisdom from

JOE COOL

ACTUALLY, WE JOE
COOLS ARE SCARED TO
DEATH OF CHICKS.

THE IMPORTANCE OF

Good Sportsmanship

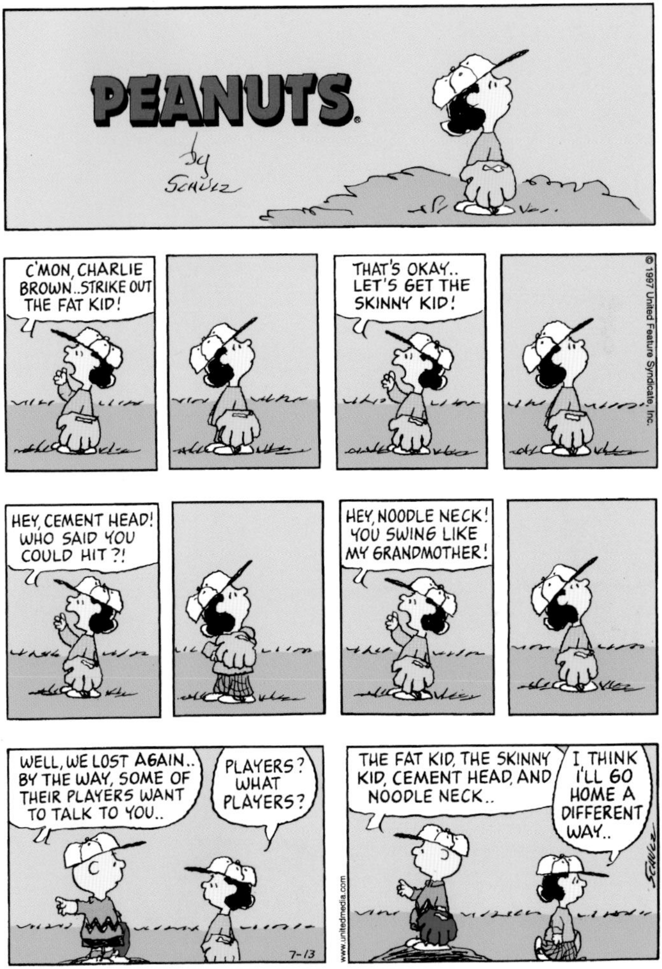
PEANUTS
by SCHULZ
C'MON, CHARLIE BROWN..STRIKE OUT THE FAT KID!
THAT'S OKAY.. LET'S GET THE SKINNY KID!
© 1997 United Feature Syndicate, Inc.
HEY, CEMENT HEAD! WHO SAID YOU COULD HIT?!
HEY, NOODLE NECK! YOU SWING LIKE MY GRANDMOTHER!
WELL, WE LOST AGAIN.. BY THE WAY, SOME OF THEIR PLAYERS WANT TO TALK TO YOU..
PLAYERS? WHAT PLAYERS?
7-13
www.unitedmedia.com
THE FAT KID, THE SKINNY KID, CEMENT HEAD, AND NOODLE NECK..
I THINK I'LL GO HOME A DIFFERENT WAY..
SCHULZ

How to tell a turtle from a hubcap...

FOR "SHOW AND TELL" THIS MORNING I HAVE A TURTLE WHICH I SAVED WHEN IT WAS TRYING TO CROSS THE ROAD..
© 1993 United Feature Syndicate, Inc.
3-4
IT ISN'T?
FOR "SHOW AND TELL" THIS MORNING I HAVE A HUBCAP WHICH I SAVED WHEN IT WAS TRYING TO CROSS THE ROAD..
SCHULZ

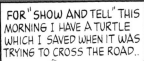

IF YOU HAVE ENJOYED THIS BOOK, WE WOULD LOVE TO HEAR FROM YOU.

PLEASE SEND YOUR COMMENTS TO:

Hallmark Book Feedback
P.O. Box 419034
Mail Drop 215
Kansas City, MO 64141

OR E-MAIL US AT:

booknotes@hallmark.com

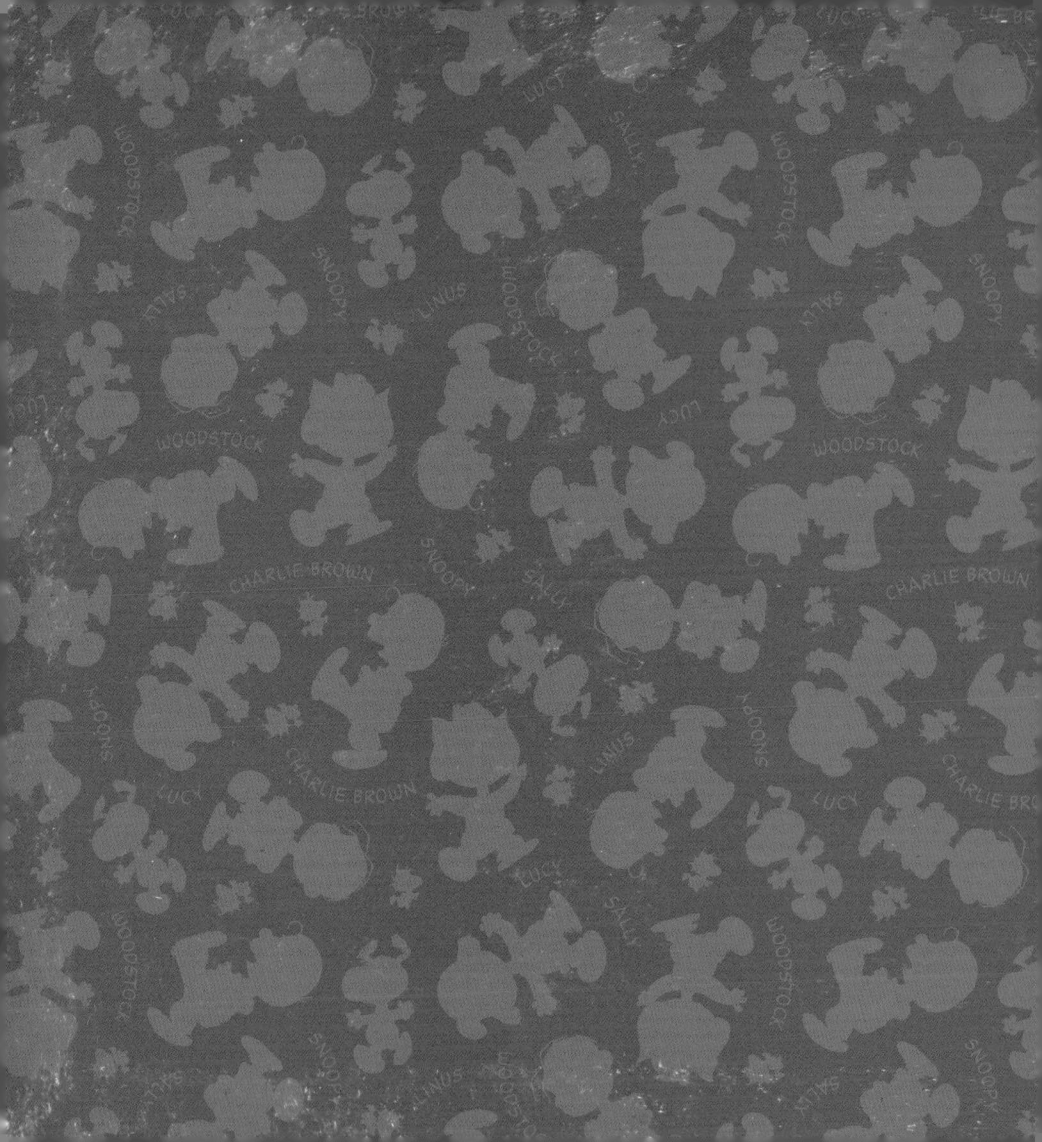
WOODSTOCK
SNOOPY
SALLY
LINUS
LUCY
CHARLIE BROWN